VICTORIA FALLS

Anna Rebus

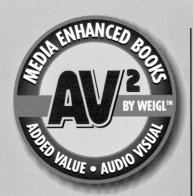

Go to www.av2books.com, and enter this book's unique code.

BOOK CODE

A V J 7 5 5 9 8

AV² by Weigl brings you media enhanced books that support active learning.

AV² provides enriched content that supplements and complements this book. Weigl's AV² books strive to create inspired learning and engage young minds in a total learning experience.

Your AV² Media Enhanced books come alive with...

Audio
Listen to sections of the book read aloud.

Key Words
Study vocabulary, and complete a matching word activity.

Video
Watch informative video clips.

Quizzes
Test your knowledge.

Embedded Weblinks
Gain additional information for research.

Slideshow
View images and captions, and prepare a presentation.

Try This!
Complete activities and hands-on experiments.

... and much, much more!

Published by AV² by Weigl
350 5th Avenue, 59th Floor
New York, NY 10118
Website: www.av2books.com

Library of Congress Control Number: 2019938447

ISBN 978-1-7911-0862-5 (hardcover)
ISBN 978-1-7911-0863-2 (softcover)
ISBN 978-1-7911-0864-9 (multi-user eBook)
ISBN 978-1-7911-0865-6 (single-user eBook)

Printed in Guangzhou, China
1 2 3 4 5 6 7 8 9 23 22 21 20 19

052019
311018

Project Coordinator Heather Kissock
Design Ana Maria Vidal and Tammy West

Every reasonable effort has been made to trace ownership and to obtain permission to reprint copyright material. The publishers would be pleased to have any errors or omissions brought to their attention so that they may be corrected in subsequent printings.

Photo Credits
Weigl acknowledges Getty Images, Alamy, and iStock as primary photo suppliers for this title.

VICTORIA FALLS

Contents

A Wealth of Life

At more than 5,500 feet (1,700 meters) wide and 355 feet (108 m) high, Victoria Falls in southern Africa is the largest curtain of falling water in the world. It is so large that at times the spray from the falls rises to a height of 1,300 feet (400 m) and is visible 30 miles (50 kilometers) away.

A wealth of plants and animals live in the Victoria Falls area. Some of the land on either side of the falls is preserved as national parks. Many large mammals live in the parks, including rare white rhinoceroses, cheetahs, hippopotamuses, wildebeests, and elephants. Smaller animals include birds, otters, wild dogs, and warthogs. There are also many **species** of plants. Some of these plants can be eaten, while others are used as medicine.

Moonbows, which are like rainbows but come from the light of the Moon reflecting on the water, can be seen at Victoria Falls.

The chacma, or Cape, baboon is often seen in the Victoria Falls region. It is one of the largest types of monkey.

Victoria Falls Facts

- Victoria Falls is one-and-a-half times as wide and twice as high as North America's Niagara Falls.

- Victoria Falls is on the Zambezi River in southern Africa.

- The Zambezi River is about 2,200 miles (3,540 km) long and is the fourth longest river in Africa.

- Between February and April each year, the Zambezi River is in full flood. Every minute, about 110 million gallons (500 million liters) of water flow over Victoria Falls.

- The locals call Victoria Falls *Mosi-Oa-Tunya*, or "the smoke that thunders."

- In November, the water level of the Zambezi River is low. About 2.64 million gallons (10 million liters) of water flow over the falls each minute.

Mapping Victoria Falls

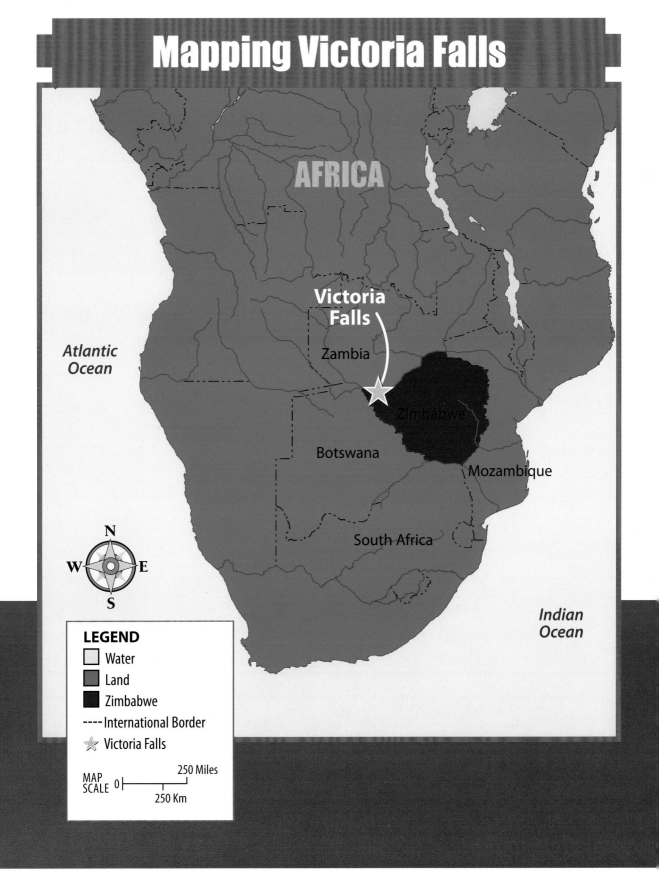

AFRICA

Atlantic
Ocean

Victoria
Falls

Zambia

Zimbabwe

Botswana

Mozambique

South Africa

Indian
Ocean

N
W   E
S

LEGEND
- Water
- Land
- Zimbabwe
- - - - International Border
- ⭐ Victoria Falls

MAP
SCALE   0 |————————| 250 Miles
            250 Km

Where in the World?

Victoria Falls is located on the Zambezi River, which forms a natural border between the countries of Zambia and Zimbabwe. The Zambezi River also flows through Angola, Namibia, Botswana, and Mozambique. Along the way, smaller rivers feed into the Zambezi. During the rainy season between November and March, massive amounts of water flow along the mighty Zambezi.

Directly opposite Victoria Falls is a lush forest. The falls and their surrounding area are so important that they have been declared a **UNESCO World Heritage Site**. Located 6 miles (10 km) away from the falls, the town of Livingstone is home to more than 100,000 people. About 8,000 people live in the nearby traditional Mukuni Village.

People in Mukuni Village live in huts with either thatched or metal roofs.

Hippopotamuses can spend up to 16 hours per day in the water of the Zambezi River.

Puzzler

Victoria Falls is on the Zambezi River in Africa. This river flows through six countries before reaching the Indian Ocean. **Where are these countries located? Find each one on the map. Also find the Indian Ocean.**

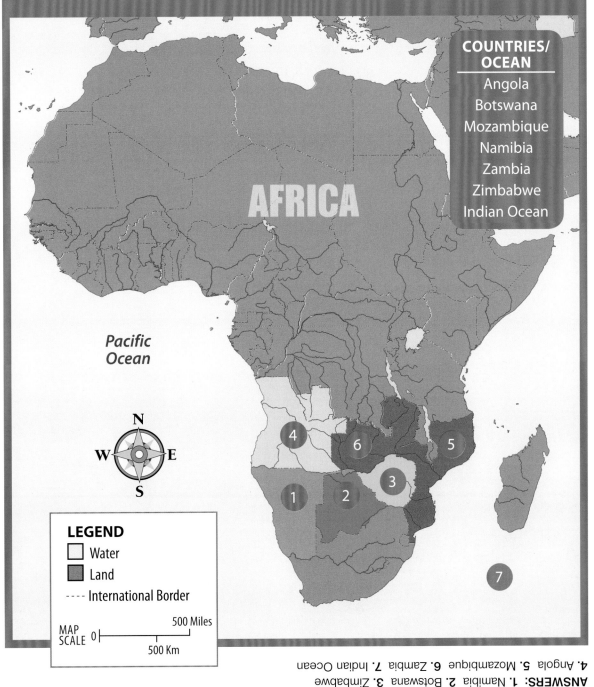

COUNTRIES/ OCEAN

Angola
Botswana
Mozambique
Namibia
Zambia
Zimbabwe
Indian Ocean

AFRICA

Pacific Ocean

N
W E
S

LEGEND
☐ Water
☐ Land
---- International Border

MAP SCALE 0 |——————| 500 Miles
           |——————|
              500 Km

A Trip Back in Time

The region around Victoria Falls began to form millions of years ago. The falls themselves are a result of several natural events. These include volcanic activity, erosion, and the flow of the Zambezi River.

The Victoria Falls area stands on a volcanic layer of rock called basalt. Millions of years ago, a vast inland sea covered what is today the northern part of Botswana. As the sea water levels went down, fine **sediments** were deposited on top of the basalt. The Zambezi River has slowly cut its way through the layers of basalt and sediments. From the air above the falls, a series of cracks in the land can be seen. This shows that the river has changed its course through time.

The Zambezi River continues to shape the land to this day. Above the falls, the river is wide and flows around islands. It then plunges over the falls into a series of deep **gorges**.

Zambezi means "Great River" in one of the local languages.

The Running River

The Zambezi River is divided into upper, middle, and lower river sections. Victoria Falls marks the boundary between the upper and middle Zambezi.

The Upper River
The Zambezi River has its **source** in the country of Zambia. In this section, the river is joined by many smaller rivers, or tributaries. The river becomes wider as more water from these tributaries flows into it.

The Middle River
After the water plunges over Victoria Falls, the river runs for around 600 miles (966 km). Two dams have been built on the middle river that generate **hydroelectric** power. Kariba Dam was completed in 1959. Cahora Bassa Dam opened in 1974. Each dam has created a reservoir, or lake.

The Lower River
From Cahora Bassa Dam, the Zambezi River makes its way to the Indian Ocean. This section of the river is about 400 miles (650 km) long. The delta of the Zambezi is where the river meets the ocean.

The Kariba Dam is 420 feet (128 m) tall and 1,900 feet (579 m) long. It formed Lake Kariba.

Plentiful Plants

A cloud of mist is produced as water plunges over Victoria Falls. The mist has created a rainforest opposite the falls, where ebony, mahogany, and fig trees grow. This forest remains lush even when the surrounding countryside is very dry.

A number of important plant species are found around Victoria Falls. One of these, the tree fern, grows throughout southern Africa. It usually reaches heights of between 6.5 and 10 feet (2 and 3 m). Some tree ferns can grow up to 26 feet (8 m) tall. Scientists believe that the tree fern could become rare in the wild.

The flame lily is the national flower of Zimbabwe. It blooms in December in the rainforests near Victoria Falls.

Not all plants at Victoria Falls have been there for long. Some were brought to the Victoria Falls area by early European settlers. Many have become pest plants. Lantana is a pretty plant, but it spreads quickly and poisons cattle.

During the rainy season, the rainforest can experience multiple days in a row of constant rain.

The Rainy Season

The volume of water in the Zambezi River changes throughout the seasons. The amount of water in the Zambezi River affects the amount of water going over Victoria Falls. This region experiences rainy and dry seasons every year.

The rainy season occurs between November and March when the weather becomes very hot and humid. Between February and April, the Zambezi River is in full flood. There is so much spray rising up from Victoria Falls that it can be difficult to get a good view of the falls from the ground. During the rainy season, storms form suddenly and are followed quickly by sunshine and blue skies.

The dry season occurs between April and October. By September and October, there is much less water going over the falls and much less spray. Visitors can clearly see the cliff edge that the water plunges over.

The roaring noise of Victoria Falls can be heard from almost 25 miles (40 km) away.

Zambezi Animals

S ome amazing animals live near Victoria Falls. Large mammals, such as lions, elephants, zebras, giraffes, and rhinoceroses, roam across the land. Grazing animals, such as antelopes and impalas, must keep a careful eye out for hunting cheetahs. These big cats are the fastest mammals on Earth.

More than 400 species of bird live in the Victoria Falls area. The Zambezi River Basin, of which Victoria Falls is part, is home to 95 percent of the world's wattled cranes. Fewer than 10,000 wattled cranes remain in southern Africa.

The wattled crane is the largest crane in Africa.

Scientists have found 84 species of fish in the waters above the falls, while 39 species of fish have been recorded below the falls. Some fish are very large. The giant vundu is a type of catfish. It can grow to more than 6 feet (1.8 m) long and weigh up to 132 pounds (60 kilograms).

Elephants need to keep their skin moist. They wade in the Zambezi River near the falls to do so.

Endangered Species

In southern Africa, many plants and animal species are in danger of becoming extinct. Being extinct means that a certain species no longer exists. Humans are often to blame for plant and animal extinctions. People need places to live, but in the process of building homes, they destroy important **habitat**. Along the Zambezi River, dams have been built. As a result, some habitats have been flooded, while others have dried out.

Zambia once had a large population of rhinoceroses, but they were hunted by **poachers** to near extinction for their horns. A few white rhinoceroses have been brought from other countries into Mosi-Oa-Tunya National Park near Victoria Falls. However, some of them have died. Poachers have also hunted elephants for their tusks. Some herds of elephants and rhinoceroses are now guarded by rangers.

Only 10 white rhinoceroses were living in Mosi-Oa-Tunya National Park as of 2018. About 20,000 white rhinoceroses live elsewhere in Africa.

Researching the Falls

Scientists study Victoria Falls in different ways. Studying water samples taken from the falls area tells scientists if pollution is entering the river farther upstream. Photographs of the falls taken from an airplane can help researchers understand how the rocks have eroded over time.

Scientists know that Victoria Falls, the Zambezi River, and the surrounding land exist in a delicate balance. The survival of local plants and animals and their habitats can be affected by drought, floods, fire, and human settlement. Two large hydroelectric dams have been built along the Zambezi River. While they provide power for people, dams upset the normal flow of water. Researchers study how the dams have affected the natural environment.

Scientists are working on a way to make the water released from the Cahora Bassa Dam act more like the natural flow of the Zambezi River.

Droughts can cause almost no water to flow over the falls.

Biography

David Livingstone (1813–1873)

David Livingstone devoted much of his life to exploring the continent of Africa. Livingstone was a doctor and missionary turned explorer. He traveled 29,000 miles (47,000 km) in Africa. In 1855, he became the first European to see and describe Victoria Falls, which he named after Queen Victoria of Great Britain.

In 1866, Livingstone set out to find the source of Africa's Nile River. Having no contact with the outside world for several years, Livingstone was feared dead. Henry Stanley, a journalist for the *New York Herald*, was sent to find Livingstone. Stanley reached Livingstone in November 1871 and uttered the now famous phrase, "Dr. Livingstone, I presume?"

David Livingstone wrote the book *Missionary Travels and Researches in South Africa* in 1857, after he returned to Great Britain from the trip where he first saw Victoria Falls.

Facts of Life

- Born: March 19, 1813
- Hometown: Blantyre, Lanarkshire, Scotland
- Occupation: Doctor, missionary, explorer
- Died: May 1, 1873

The Big Picture

The Zambezi River is one of many great river systems found throughout the world. Rivers provide important habitats for animals. Towns and cities are often built near rivers. People use rivers as a source of drinking water and food, as transportation routes, as a place for leisure activities, and to generate hydroelectricity.

North America

Atlantic Ocean

Pacific Ocean

South America

LEGEND

Water
Land
River

N
W   E
S

MAP SCALE 0 |————————| 2,000 Miles
                    2,000 Km

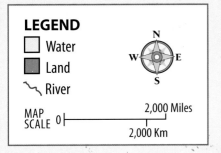

Mississippi River
North America

Amazon River
South America

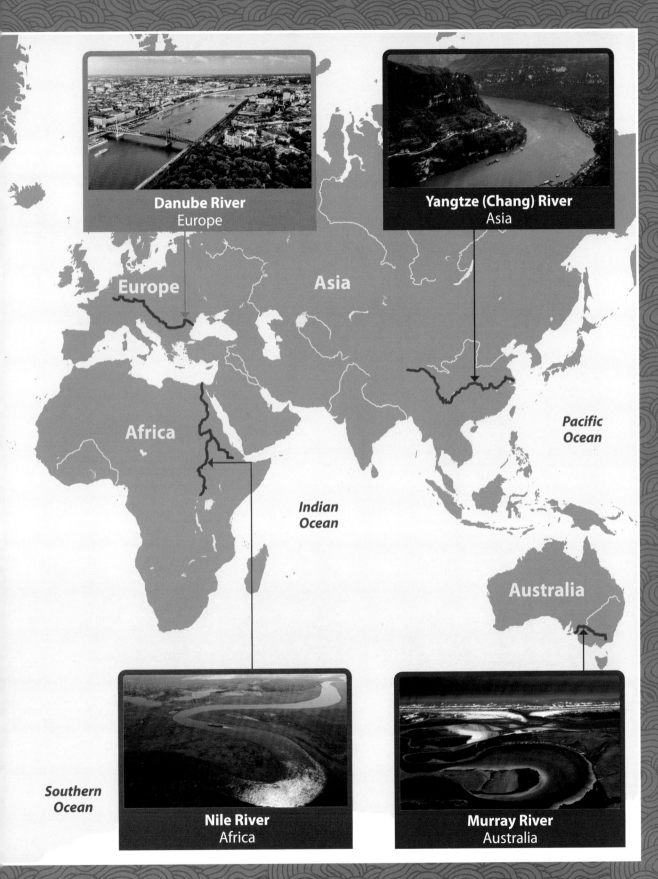

Danube River
Europe

Yangtze (Chang) River
Asia

Europe

Asia

Africa

Pacific Ocean

Indian Ocean

Australia

Southern Ocean

Nile River
Africa

Murray River
Australia

People of the Falls

People have lived in the Victoria Falls area for a very long time. Stone tools used by early **hominids** have been found. They date back to 2 million years ago. Digging tools and weapons have also been discovered that tell us **hunter-gatherers** lived in the area between 2,000 and 10,000 years ago. After that time, people near Victoria Falls began living in villages, using iron tools, and raising livestock.

Ndebele women wear copper and brass rings around their arms, neck, and legs as a sign of their position in society.

Today, there is a mix of people and cultures living near Victoria Falls. The Tonga people have lived in the area for at least 700 years, along with Toka, Leya, Subiya, and Totela people. By the mid-1800s, a people called the Makololo also lived here. They called the falls *Mosi-Oa-Tunya*, meaning "the smoke that thunders." Ndebele people and people of European **ancestry** are more recent arrivals.

Some of the peoples in the Victoria Falls region dress in elaborate costumes as part of traditional dances and ceremonies.

Puzzler

Baobab trees grow near Victoria Falls. The baobab is an unusual tree. It only has leaves for three months of the year. During the other nine months, it stores water in its thick trunk. Baobab trees grow in many other places, too. **In which parts of the world do baobab trees grow?**

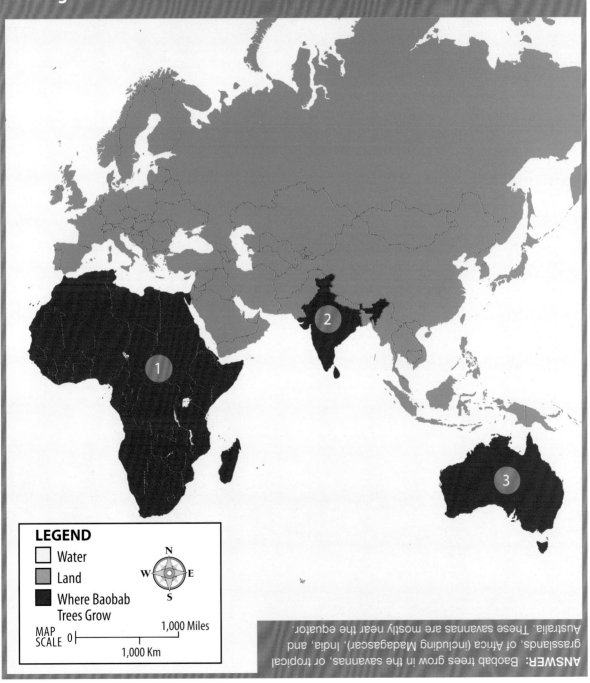

LEGEND
- ☐ Water
- ☐ Land
- ■ Where Baobab Trees Grow

MAP SCALE
0 — 1,000 Miles
1,000 Km

ANSWER: Baobab trees grow in the savannas, or tropical grasslands, of Africa (including Madagascar), India, and Australia. These savannas are mostly near the equator.

Victoria Falls 19

Timeline

2 million years ago
Hominids, the ancestors of early humans, live near Victoria Falls.

1200s
The village of Gundu is founded near Victoria Falls. It is later renamed Mukuni Village.

2 million years ago	2,000 years ago	1200s	1700	1800	1900

2,000 years ago
People begin living in villages near Victoria Falls. They use iron tools and keep livestock.

1905
The Victoria Falls Bridge is opened.

1855
David Livingstone is the first European to see and describe Victoria Falls.

2018
The number of tourists increases in the area, following $150 million of upgrades to Victoria Falls International Airport in 2017.

1969–1974
Construction of the Cahora Bassa Dam on the Zambezi River takes place.

1989
Mosi-Oa-Tunya and Victoria Falls National Parks are listed as a UNESCO World Heritage Site.

1920	1935	1950	1965	1980	1995	2010

1955–1959
Kariba Dam is constructed on the Zambezi River.

1972
Victoria Falls becomes a national park 38 years after it was first made a protected area.

Disappearing Habitat

People travel from all over the world to see the spectacular Victoria Falls. Visitors need hotels to stay in, roads to travel on, and activities to do. All of this development means the land is no longer left in its natural state. Once another road or hotel is built, animals can no longer roam free in that area. On the other hand, visitors spend money that helps support the local economy and provides people with jobs.

The Victoria Falls Railway Station opened in 1904. Visitors can still travel by train to Victoria Falls today.

Finding a balance between promoting tourism and protecting the environment is very difficult. More visitors mean more land is cleared for development. Habitat is lost, and some animals in this area have become endangered. Land on either side of Victoria Falls has been protected from development by being declared a national park.

NOTICE
YOU ARE ENTERING NATIONAL PARKS LAND. PLEASE LOOK OUT FOR WILD ANIMALS. THANK YOU.

Signs at Victoria Falls National Park remind visitors that the land is first and foremost home to wild animals.

Should more development be allowed at Victoria Falls?

Yes	No
Tourism gives local people jobs and money. People can buy homes and send their children to school.	More development will mean there is less habitat for animals.
More roads and hotels mean more people can experience the beauty of the falls.	Visitors create pollution, use precious natural resources, and leave behind garbage.
Land can be set aside as national parks where development can be controlled.	Some of the hotels and shops are not owned by people in the local area. The money the owners make does not go back into the local economy.

The Victoria Falls Safari Lodge, which opened in 1994, was built to look like traditional housing in the area. However, it is seven stories tall and has modern features like swimming pools.

Natural Attractions

Each year, more than 1 million tourists visit Victoria Falls. Tourists spend money on food, hotels, and souvenirs. This money helps to support the local community and provides people with jobs.

Tourists can view the falls in different ways. Just below the falls, the Victoria Falls Bridge carries trains, cars, and foot traffic. Some people take flights over the falls in helicopters or small planes. A series of walking trails allows visitors to get so close to the falls that they get wet from the spray. In the park around the falls, visitors can go on **safari** and get a close-up view of animals such as lions, elephants, rhinoceroses, and zebras in their natural habitat.

During the rainy season, whitewater rafters must start farther from the base of Victoria Falls because the water flow is too high to be safe.

Local people sell souvenirs to tourists as a source of income.

Be Prepared

A visit to Victoria Falls can be a challenge. However, with proper preparation, it can be a once-in-a-lifetime experience.

Expect hot weather most of the year. In winter (June and July), be prepared for warm days and cooler evenings.

Spray from the falls will soak your clothes. Bring a raincoat or poncho to keep your clothes and camera dry.

There are hundreds of types of birds living in the Victoria Falls area. A bird book will help you identify the various species.

Bring a pair of binoculars to view the animals you will see while on safari.

Plan to wear sturdy shoes for hiking near the falls or going on a safari walk.

Always drink plenty of water to prevent dehydration, or drying out. Drink bottled water.

Use plenty of insect repellent. Mosquitoes transmit malaria, a disease that causes chills, sweating, and fever.

Local Knowledge

Over thousands of years, people living near Victoria Falls have gathered knowledge about local plants. They know which species are poisonous and which are safe to eat.

A plant may be useful in many different ways. Various parts of the baobab tree have different uses. The inner bark is made into a strong rope. The seedpods are used to carry liquids. The fruit pulp is mixed with water to create a refreshing drink. Young leaves are used in soups, and the seeds can be roasted and eaten.

The main seeds grown in Zimbabwe are maize, soybean, cotton, and sorghum. Once harvested, the seeds are sorted by hand before selling or eating.

Some plants can also be used to treat ailments, including skin irritations and stomach upsets. The leaves, roots, and bark of the African ebony and Cape fig trees are used in traditional medicine. The fruits and leaves of the Cape fig are also given to cattle to make them produce more milk.

People can eat Cape fig fruit either fresh or dried.

Sacred Ceremony

Located near Victoria Falls, Mukuni Village is home to 8,000 people. Mukuni villagers belong to the Toka-Leya culture. Victoria Falls is an important and sacred place for the Toka-Leya people. They believe that the spirits of their ancestors dwell around the falls. Each year before the rains come, the Lwiindi ceremony is performed in a hut near the village graveyard. A sacred drum is played, and villagers pray to their ancestors to make the rains come. After the ceremony, the villagers feast, dance, and sing.

The Mukuni villagers hold the Kuomboka ceremony at the end of the rainy season, when the river has risen.

What Have You Learned?

True or False?

Decide whether the following statements are true or false. If the statement is false, make it true.

1. In 1755, David Livingstone became the first European to see Victoria Falls.

2. Victoria Falls is the largest curtain of falling water in the world.

3. Elephants are hunted by poachers for their hide.

4. The spray from Victoria Falls can be seen 250 miles (400 km) away.

5. The Danube River is in Africa.

6. The dry season in Zambia occurs between April and October.

ANSWERS: 1. False. He saw the falls in 1855. **2.** True **3.** False. Elephants are killed for their ivory tusks. **4.** False. The spray can be seen up to 30 miles (50 km) away. **5.** False. The Danube River is in Europe. **6.** True

Short Answer

Answer the following questions using information from the book.

1. Victoria Falls is found on the border of which two countries?

2. The Zambezi River flows through which countries?

3. What is the name of the ceremony performed at Mukuni Village to make the rains come?

4. How long is the Zambezi River?

5. Victoria Falls is what type of UNESCO site?

ANSWERS: 1. Zambia and Zimbabwe **2.** Angola, Namibia, Botswana, Zambia, Zimbabwe, and Mozambique **3.** Lwiindi ceremony **4.** About 2,200 miles (3,540 km) long **5.** World Heritage Site

Multiple Choice

Choose the best answer for the following questions.

1. The local name for Victoria Falls, Mosi-Oa-Tunya, means:

a. "the mist that is wet"
b. "the smoke that thunders"
c. "the falling water"
d. "the river falls away"

2. Which cultural group lives at Mukuni Village near Victoria Falls?

a. The Cree
b. The Hopi
c. The Inca
d. The Toka-Leya

3. One of the two dams on the Zambezi River is called the Cahora Bassa Dam. What is the other one called?

a. The Hoover Dam
b. The Aswan High Dam
c. The Kariba Dam
d. The Three Gorges Dam

4. When the last member of a species dies, it is said to be:

a. rare
b. abundant
c. threatened
d. extinct

ANSWERS: 1. b 2. d 3. c 4. d

Activity

Building a Bridge

The Victoria Falls Bridge is 650 feet (198 m) long and 400 feet (122 m) above the Zambezi River. It took 14 months to complete. The Victoria Falls Bridge is used by trains, automobiles, and pedestrians. Try this activity to see how strong a bridge you can build.

Materials

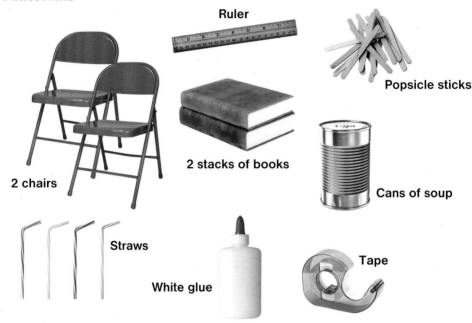

Ruler

Popsicle sticks

2 chairs

2 stacks of books

Cans of soup

Straws

White glue

Tape

Instructions

1. Place two chairs 16 inches (41 centimeters) apart.

2. Use any combination of the Popsicle sticks, straws, glue, and tape to build a strong bridge 20 inches (50 cm) long so that each side will be 2 inches (5 cm) on the chair and supported by books.

3. Test how many soup cans your bridge can support before collapsing.

Results

You will see the strength of your bridge. If you repeated this experiment, what would you do to make it stronger? Are there other materials that you would use?

Key Words

ancestry: people from the past who are related to people today

gorges: narrow and deep passages that cut through rock

habitat: the environment where a plant or animal is normally found

hominids: the ancient ancestors of humans

hunter-gatherers: people that survive by hunting for animals and collecting plants to eat

hydroelectric: related to the production of electricity that is created by the flow of running water

poachers: people who illegally hunt animals

safari: a trip that people take to view animals in their natural environment

sediments: silt and sand that is carried or deposited by a flowing river or body of water

source: the place where a river starts

species: a specific group of plants or animals that share the same characteristics

UNESCO World Heritage Site: a place that is of natural or cultural importance to the entire world. UNESCO is an abbreviation for United Nations Educational, Scientific, and Cultural Organization.

Index

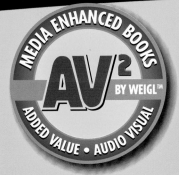

Log on to www.av2books.com

AV² by Weigl brings you media enhanced books that support active learning. Go to www.av2books.com, and enter the special code found on page 2 of this book. You will gain access to enriched and enhanced content that supplements and complements this book. Content includes video, audio, weblinks, quizzes, a slideshow, and activities.

AV² Online Navigation

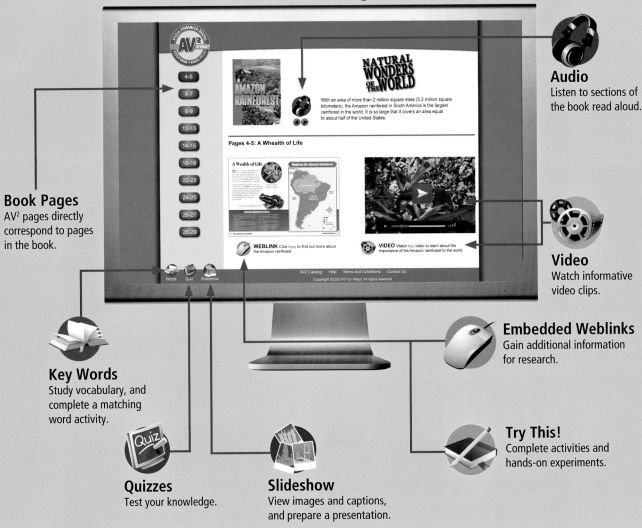

Audio
Listen to sections of the book read aloud.

Book Pages
AV² pages directly correspond to pages in the book.

Video
Watch informative video clips.

Key Words
Study vocabulary, and complete a matching word activity.

Embedded Weblinks
Gain additional information for research.

Try This!
Complete activities and hands-on experiments.

Quizzes
Test your knowledge.

Slideshow
View images and captions, and prepare a presentation.

AV² was built to bridge the gap between print and digital. We encourage you to tell us what you like and what you want to see in the future.

Sign up to be an AV² Ambassador at www.av2books.com/ambassador.